Generis

PUBLISHING

Is the Australian housing market in a bubble?

Dr. Justine Wang
Dr. John S. Croucher

Title: Is the Australian housing market in a bubble?

ISBN: 978-1-63902-259-5

Author: Dr. Justine Wang, Dr. John S. Croucher

Cover image: www.pixabay.com

Publisher: Generis Publishing
Online orders: www.generis-publishing.com
Contact email: info@generis-publishing.com

Table of Contents

Abstract

Purpose – This paper aims to explore principal drivers affecting prices in the Australian housing market, aiming to detect the presence of housing bubbles within it. The data set analyzed covers the past two decades, thereby including the period of the most recent pre-pandemic housing boom started in 2012.

Design/methodology/approach – The paper describes the application of combined enhanced rigorous econometric frameworks, such as ordinary least square (OLS), Granger causality and the Vector Error Correction Model (VECM) framework, to provide an in-depth understanding of house price dynamics and bubbles in Australia.

Findings – The empirical results presented reveal that Australian house prices are driven primarily by four key factors: mortgage interest rates, consumer sentiment, the Australian S&P/ASX 200 stock market index and unemployment rates. It finds that these four key drivers have long-term equilibrium in relation to house prices, and any short-term disequilibrium always self-corrects over the long term because of economic forces. The existence of long-term equilibrium in the housing market suggests it is unlikely to be in a bubble (Diba and Grossman, 1988; Flood and Hodrick, 1986).

Originality/value – The foremost contribution of this paper is that it is the first rigorous study of housing bubbles in Australia at the national level. Additionally, the data set renders the study of particular interest because it incorporates an analysis of the most recent pre-pandemic housing boom started in 2012 due to the concerns and risks associated with the current pandemic housing boom which grows at the fastest annual pace since 1989. The policy implications from the study arise from the discussion of how best to balance monetary policy, fiscal policy and macroeconomic policy to optimize the steady and stable growth of the Australian housing market, and from its reconsideration of affordability schemes and related policies designed to incentivize construction and the involvement of complementary industries associated with property.

Introduction

According to estimates, approximately 57 per cent of Australia's wealth is concentrated in residential properties (CoreLogic, 2021). Thus, changes to house prices have a notable impact on the Australian economy overall, and particularly on investment options and wealth management. In the case of the majority of mortgages and many small businesses, credit and mortgage debt are secured against residential properties. Consequently, property plays a critical role in securitisation, with responsibility for backing financial institutions' financial positioning statements (Kohler and Merwe, 2015).

The large proportion of credit secured against properties and mortgage debt expenditure are both closely correlated with short-term interest rates, especially because variable rate contracts are prevalent within the mortgage market (Koblyakova *et al.*, 2014). As a result, Aron and Muellbauer (2010) explain that changes to mortgage policy rates pose a threat to financial stability. In the period from October 2012 to September 2015, there were six consecutive cuts in cash base rates by the Reserve Bank of Australia (RBA), prompting concerns that the Australian housing market might be highly vulnerable to the transmission of monetary policy changes on a cash basis because the Australian market has an outstanding stock of residential mortgage debt to gross domestic product (GDP) ratio of 78 per cent (ABS, 2016a, 2016b; RBA, 2016). Thus, this figure implies that changes in mortgage interest rate would be expected to have a significant impact on Australia's economic output and stability of the financial system.

Research considering opportunities to maintain Australia's financial stability and ensure healthy economic growth, brings into question the effectiveness of current monetary policy in view of the RBA's decision to adjust the cash base rate. For example, Kehoe (2016) argues that easy availability of debt because of the reduction in mortgage interest rates might encourage an increase in property transactions and inflate prices, a trend that would be reversed if opportunities for debt were perceived to be scarce. In view of the property industry's importance to government policy, studies to measure the influence of the property industry on Australia's economy are essential.

This is because the property market is of utmost importance to assessments of GDP, and an understanding of the main drivers of Australian house prices is crucial for key institutional agents such as financials, professional services and construction industries. In 2015, the property industry represents a total economic input of $182.8bn, i.e. 11.5 per cent of total GDP (Bleby, 2016). Therefore, the property industry, which has doubled its contribution to GDP over the past decade, has overtaken former pillar industries, including financial services and mining.

Studies conducted concerning residential property prices over the past 20 years are attracting increased attention, particularly in relation to house prices, which play a pivotal role in Australia's economy, as explained above, as well as in Australians' daily lives. Certainly, understanding house price dynamics is of great importance to the national economy, because as stated above, residential house prices impact the housing market and the past 30 years, Australian house prices have risen 7.15 per cent annually on average up to 2015 (Kohler and Merwe, 2015). Over the same period, investment in property has expanded, and property prices have passed through three cycles of peaks and troughs (Harley, 2016). In 2021, Australia has experienced a pandemic property boom with the growth at the fastest annual pace since 1989. In the most recent pre pandemic housing boom started in 2012 and current pandemic housing boom, prices soared, prompting fears about what would arise if a bubble were to develop within the market. A housing bubble could have a disastrous and widespread effect, in the form of economic recession, financial distress and loss of household wealth.

Furthermore, while house price dynamics have been explored previously (Abelson *et al.*, 2005; Bodman and Crosby, 2004; Bourassa and Hendershott, 1995; Hatzvi and Otto, 2008; Kohler and Merwe, 2015; Otto, 2007), limited empirical tests have been performed on contemporary data to understand the implications of the most recent housing boom in Australia. In previous research, few attempts have been made to test for the presence of bubbles, with the result that the main drivers of Australian house prices and the presence of housing bubbles over the past two decades are not well understood. Focusing upon sub- market analysis (Wilson *et al.*, 2011), the majority of previous studies investigating Australian house prices have been confined to data gathered in major capital cities (Abelson *et al.*, 2005; Bodman and Crosby, 2004; Hatzvi and Otto, 2008; Otto, 2007, Shi *et al.*, 2016).

Limited analysis has been performed to capture the implications of the Australian housing market at the national level (Abelson *et al.*, 2005); therefore, this research aims to address this knowledge gap by being the first to study housing bubbles in Australia at the national level. This is a very important question, as deeper understanding of the housing market issues from the national perspective may facilitate comparative analysis between the national and regionally disaggregated factors, also helping to optimize the aggregate economic and housing market performance. In its part, this research may also be useful for the Australian government aiming to assist in monitoring country's economic goals by setting appropriate key performance indicators. Another distinctive feature of this analysis is that it concentrates on the impact of current disputes and fears raised in reference to the role of large Chinese buyer purchases and the purchase of property through self-managed super funds.

This paper poses two research questions:

RQ1. What are the main drivers of Australian house prices?

RQ2. Is there a bubble in the Australian housing market?

RQ1 is asked with an understanding that house price dynamics could have diverse implications in different sectors of the Australian economy; while *RQ2* relates to the need to assess the risk of bubbles because of their potential to impact housing market instability, economic recession and housing affordability.

The remainder of this article is organized as follows. The following section reviews the most recently published studies examining house price dynamics and bubbles. The third section highlights key theoretical concepts relating to house price studies. The fourth section details the data set used, and the empirical method and processes employed to analyze the results are discussed in sections five and six, focusing on the assumptions and issues raised by each method and the respective findings. The final section of the article provides concluding comments and outlines opportunities for future research.

Literature review

This section analyzes relevant literature pertaining to both house price dynamics and housing bubbles, to provide a theoretical context in which to understand the Australian housing market, understand empirical specifications of house prices, and identify gaps in the existing literature.

The term "bubble" is widely used in reference to house prices, but it is rarely clearly defined (Case and Shiller, 2004). Exploring the determinants of house prices, and considering the risks associated with housing bubbles it is essential to understand the housing market in Australia. Fernández-Kranz and Hon (2006) suggest that a bubble arises in relation to three typical scenarios:

(1)   When in a housing bubble property prices peak.

(2)   When house prices are higher than would be expected based on a fundamental equilibrium.

(3)   When there is a sharp rise in growth because of an unexpected event prompting a market-shift.

Applying the US data for 1986-2004, Del Negro and Otrok (2005) use a dynamic model factor for exploring house price dynamics influenced by state/region specific shocks. Results suggest that historical movements in house prices have been driven by the local (state specific) components, including such fundamental regionally differentiated factors as growth rates in real per capita incomes and real wages levels. It also has been found that despite "regional bubbles" have been detected in some states in 2001-2004 period, the overall increase in house prices has occurred at the national level. Developing this topic further, Himmelberg *et al.* (2005) found a little evidence of housing bubbles in the majority of states, suggesting that although house price movements are local factors, national level data undercover important economic variations among various locations. Importantly, research suggests that changes in underlying fundamentals can impact various cities differently also showing that in locations where housing supply is relatively inelastic, house prices may typically be more sensitive to changes in interest rates. Thus, an unexpected rise in real interest rates that raises housing costs would negatively affect housing demand, possibly leading to "anti-bubble" event.

Turning attention to empirical methods used to test for bubbles; to date, related work comparing the econometric techniques applied to test bubbles are somewhat limited. Indisputably, however, an empirical analysis of housing market dynamics, and a clear understanding of the strengths and limitations of various models is important before beginning this study of housing bubble existence and potential risk. Measures and considerations reported in the literature are outlined further below.

After clarifying and reviewing definitions applied to housing bubbles, the most popular is found to relate to the long-term equilibrium price. Whereby, if the long-run equilibrium price is measured based on market fundamentals, then house prices that significantly differ from that long-run equilibrium price indicate a high probability that a bubble exists (Diba and Grossman, 1988; Flood and Hodrick, 1986). By contrast, if house prices are continuously balanced in a long-run equilibrium state, then the housing market is unlikely to be in a bubble. This finding implies that the long-run equilibrium of house prices would function as one rational measure for testing the existence of housing bubbles.

Proposing an additional measure, beyond any skepticism over policy effects, Teng *et al.* (2013) argue that when there is an unreasonable belief that house prices will increase indefinitely, and prices differ excessively from the true fundamental value of the property itself, then the housing market is in a bubble. This measure accounts for the risks associated with property investors' irrational expectations.

Significantly, views about what comprises a rational expectation pose an interesting psychological question during periods where there is housing bubble. For example, homebuyers typically believe there is minimal risk involved in property investments. They also suppose that purchasing property will always be a good investment option, despite the high costs involved. Case and Shiller (2004) demonstrate property owners' strong perception that future capital gains will far exceed current outlay. As a result, many homeowners tend to save less than they did after a property purchase than they did before buying property. However, Siegel and Thaler (1997) argue that returns on asset investment (equity) return to mean reversion over the longer term. Thus, implying that house prices will eventually revert to mean property values, instead of rising indefinitely.

Concerns over difficulties measuring fundamental house price values empirically were raised by Hui and Yue (2006). The question of what is an appropriate measure for determining the fundamental price of housing is significant as a value must be established as a baseline to ascertain the existence of bubbles. Elsewhere, Flood and Hodrick (1990) offer evidence of difficulties estimating intrinsic value because of the lack of data extending infinitely into the future. Thus, it is necessary to develop new perspectives from which to explore bubble testing.

To resolve these complications, Hui and Yue (2006) introduce the concept of "exogenous macroeconomic fundamental variables" to establish housing bubbles, to overcome the difficulty of measuring the intrinsic value of assets. Their work implies that if property prices are driven by macroeconomic fundamentals, such as the disposable income of urban households, local GDP, Stock Price Index, the stock of vacant new dwellings and if residual values raise no major diagnostic concerns, then there is no housing bubble.

Based on an Irish data set, Stevenson (2008) devised a dynamic inverted demand model to estimate house prices; an approach commonly employed in European housing literature. Its limitations include that its estimations are based on original level time series data, which could produce misleading results if the assumptions of the classical linear model are violated (Wooldridge, 2012).

Related work on diagnostic concerns posed when calculating fundamental house prices has focussed on the use of static models instead of dynamic models, which calculates the system in equilibrium, and is of time-invariant nature. Stevenson (2008) concludes that inconsistent estimates and bias result, because a static model calculates fundamental values in equilibrium so is unable to account for time dependent changes.

In an alternative approach, Teng *et al.* (2013) apply the present value in housing bubble analysis, highlighting the importance of rational expectations for housing equilibrium values and estimating the size of housing bubbles using the state space method. This approach overcomes the problem of unstable intrinsic bubble specification, implying that a bubble cannot burst as long as dividends remain positive.

Highlighting the importance of bubble detection using ex ante data, Shi (2016) and Phillips *et al.* (2013) stress the importance of using real-time methods to detect housing bubbles. Shi (2016) applies the recursive bubble detection method to the residual component, to identify bubble episodes, in research that is expected to significantly reduce the probability of false positive identification (Shi, 2016; Phillips *et al.*, 2013).

In more recent work based on Hong Kong data, Arestis et al. (2017) have decomposed house prices into fundamentals, frictions and bubble episodes for a better understanding of the evolution of house prices during the period 1996(Q3)-2013(Q3). Evidence was presented that prices in the HongKong housing market was quite above their last peak, which took place in mid-1997. Precisely, the research identified that real house prices are around a 31 per cent higher than their historical maximum value. Its contribution also modifies the original Glindro and Delloro's (201) approach by including the Christiano and Fitzgerald's (2003) filter to decompose house prices. The original Glindro and Delloro's (2010) approach by including the Christiano and Fitzgerald's (2003) filter to decompose house prices. The original Glindro and Delloro's analysis was conducted by decomposing asset prices into fundamentals, cyclical and bubble components by employing the Kalman filter. (Glindro and Delloro, 2010).

The above methods reveal a conflict regarding aspects such as econometric estimation, omission and misspecification. It is acknowledged that there may be shortcomings in the research methods proposed because of limitations influencing economic models' fit to real- world data (Leamer, 1983); thus, imperfections cannot be avoided.

Updating previous research, using data gathered in Sydney between 1991 and 2006, Hatzvi and Otto (2008) provide evidence of residential property prices in Sydney's housing market. Their findings suggest a significant proportion of the variation in property prices in western regions of Sydney cannot be explained by either rents or discount factors, suggesting a possible speculative bubble. Bodman and Crosby (2004) support these findings by presenting evidence of a quantitatively significant overvaluation of median house prices in mid-2003 in both Brisbane and Sydney.

Using data for the period from 1970 to 2003, Abelson *et al.* (2005) identify positive and statistically significant effects from long-run economic determinants on Australian house prices. Their study suggests that real house prices are determined significantly and positively by variables that include real disposable income, the consumer price index, unemployment rates, real mortgage interest rates, equity prices and housing stocks. Using data from 1979 to 1993, Bourassa and Hendershott (1995) demonstrate that anticipated changes in house prices are mainly a consequence of income and demographic factors.

According to Kohler and Merwe (2015), house prices can be determined jointly by demand and supply over the long run. Discussing application of the short run housing finance perspective, Tu (2000) suggests long run and short run real housing price determinants can differ. For instance, real income is the most important factor influencing real housing price dynamics in the long run, but it does not have a significant influence on short-run housing price fluctuations, while unemployment rates and nominal mortgage rates both have long run and short run impacts on the real national housing prices.

Exploring mortgage debt influences, as Biggs *et al.* (2010) introduced, the concept of the credit impulse, represented as the difference in the flow of credit relative to GDP growth. The empirical result show that an increase in GDP is positively correlated with the increase in mortgage lending flows. In the instance of house prices, there is a causal relationship between the acceleration of mortgage debt and rising house prices (Keen, 2011). Thus, accessibility of mortgage debt led to the more than doubled house prices in the past twenty years, suggesting that the evolution of bank credit, demand for mortgage and housing demand are driven by similar economic factors and are simultaneously determined (Keen, 2007; Arestis *et al.*, 2017).

To summarize, it is undeniable that studies of house price dynamics and bubbles will produce considerable economic benefits (Fereidouni *et al.*, 2014). Research on house price dynamics and bubble risk is generally based upon rational expectation theory and housing demand theoretical frameworks, while also integrating affordability issues and possible financial stability risks. The literature discussed above identified key demand and supply explanatory variables that can affect house prices in major capital cities. Interest rates reflect short-run housing finance issues, while demand and supply factors can have long-run impacts on house prices. Moreover, any significant mismatch between housing demand and supply is likely to increase the housing bubble risk.

To date, no studies have considered the implications of house prices at the national level in Australia. Furthermore, there is a need for empirical analysis based on data sets covering a longer period, especially they cover the most recent pre pandemic housing boom in Australia started in 2012, data for which should be subjected to further empirical testing with the ultimate aim of determining policy to minimize the risk of a housing bubble developing. The issue of house price dynamics and the potential for housing bubbles in Australia at the national level needs to be re-evaluated.

Theoretical framework

The theoretical framework for house price dynamics and bubble studies used in this research was developed from rational expectation theory and the theory of housing demand. According to rational expectation theory, any outcome depends partly on expectations of what will happen. Many studies of bubbles are based on rational expectation theory (Flood and Hodrick, 1990; Kim and Suh, 1993; Chan et al., 2001; Mikhed and Zemcik, 2009). Hou (2010) states that the theoretical model for rational expectation in housing bubble analysis assesses whether a housing bubble exists by calculating the deviation between observed house prices and rational expectations of price. However, irrationality can arise when people make purchase decisions, as factors such as personal preferences and aspirations come in to play, overriding financial interest because of potential property owners' strong belief that future capital gains will result in prices far beyond what they are paying (Case and Shiller, 2004). Further, forces such as herding and frenzies can inform investors' tendency to buy or sell in the direction of a market trend (Glaeser and Nathanson, 2014), creating a self-fulfilling prophecy because of positive feedback between belief and behaviour (Shiller, 2000).

According to the theory of housing demand, a lesser amount of space or number of units is demanded when prices become higher. The central idea of housing demand suggests that effective market demand is backed by purchasing power (Arestis et al., 2017) Thus, demand for residential property obeys the fundamental law of demand (Sivitanidou, 2011).

However, a useful distinction in the demand factors that drive house price dynamics lies between longer-term and short-term influences. Long-term factors incorporate such fundamentals as demographics, household income and the tax regime (Tsatsaronis and Zhu, 2004; Meen, 2011). In a short run, the institutional structure of the housing finance system and prevailing mortgage lending conditions affects volatility in house prices via the cost of mortgage credits and availability of mortgage funds (Whitehead and Williams, 2011; Scanlon and Whitehead, 2011). Thus, when informing an empirical analysis for housing demand, these models suggest that macroeconomic, demographic, income, mortgage pricing and mortgage pricing factors are the important determinants of housing demands. A number of studies have also presented evidence that these key determinants simultaneously impact mortgage/housing demand and changes in house prices (Kohler and Merwe, 2015; Abelson et al., 2005; Otto, 2007)

Econometric methodology and specification

In this paper, we combine advanced time series empirical econometric models, as Abelson *et al.* (2005) suggest, but following two extensions. First, our study models main house price drivers at Australia's national level, while previous studies were conducted in major capital cities in Australia (Abelson *et al.*, 2005; Bodman and Crosby, 2004; Otto, 2007; Bourassa and Hendershott, 1995). Second, a combination of econometric methods is used to model house prices in both correlations and causal dimensions (Nanda and Tiwari, 2013).

The econometric specifications provide a basis for the empirical testing of house price dynamics. The estimation techniques are ordinary least squares (OLS) [equation (1)] and co- integration techniques, such as vector error correction models (VECMs); Equation (2), Equations (3) and (4) portray the empirical expressions of the models where the theoretical variables are estimated:

$$Y_i = \beta_0 + \beta_1 X_1 + \beta_2 X_2 + \beta_3 X_3 + \ldots + \beta_i X_i + Y_i\,(-1) + \mu_1. \tag{1}$$

In equation (1), house price Y_i is a function of one lag of the Y_i variable and a set of independent variables X_i. β_0 is the intercept, and β_i represents the parameter estimates. Equation (1) is an autoregressive (AR) model, which specifies that the output variable depends linearly on its own previous values and on a stochastic term. The variable μ_i describes the error term or disturbance. It contains factors other than X_i that affect Y_i (Croucher, 2017; Wooldridge, 2012):

$$\Delta Y_t = \alpha_0 + \gamma_0 D X_t + \delta(Y_{t-1} - \beta_0 X_{t-1}) + \mu_i \tag{2}$$

In equation (2), if ΔY_t and ΔX_t are I (1) processes and are *not* co-integrated, we estimate a dynamic VECM model using first differences. The first difference for house price ΔY is a function of the short-term impact of change in ΔX_t, as represented by γ_0. Long-run gravitation toward equilibrium in the relationships between variables is represented by δ. Random shocks to the system are denoted as μ_i, when $\delta < 0$ reflects the speed of the error correction term's (ECT's) work to push short-term disequilibrium in house prices to revert towards equilibrium (Wooldridge, 2012):

$$HP = \beta_0 + \beta_1 IR + \beta_2 CS + \beta_3 AUSHARE + \beta_4 UNEMPLOY + \beta_5 HP(-1) + \mu \qquad (3)$$

House prices (HP) are influenced by various macroeconomic variables (Abelson *et al.*, 2005). According to the OLS specification in equation (3), HP is a function of one lag in HP and a number of explanatory variables, including the mortgage interest rate (IR), unemployment rate (UNEMPLOY), consumer sentiment (CS) and Australian S&P/ASX 200 stock market index (AUSHARE):

$$\Delta \ln(HP_t) = \alpha_0 + \gamma_0 \Delta \ln(X_t) + \delta(\ln(HP_{t-1}) - \beta_0 \ln(X_{t-1}))_+ \mu_t \qquad (4)$$

The empirical specifications for the VECM equations are given by equation (4). In the case of the VECM model, when the error correction coefficient δ is negative and very significant, it induces a positive change in house prices back towards equilibrium (Wooldridge, 2012). Appearing as a dependent variable in the VECM equation (4), the first difference in the transformed natural logarithmic values of house price $(\ln(HP_t))$ is proxied by the first differences for the transformed natural logarithmic values of the four key macroeconomic variables $(\ln(X_t))$, namely, IR, UNEMPLOY, CS and AUSHARE. Macroeconomic variables may be used as a property explanatory argument for VECM model of house prices (Adams and Füss, 2010). According to our econometric estimates, if the long-run equilibrium of house prices is corrected through the short-run disequilibrium of these key drivers of Australian house prices, the deviation is then temporary and house price equilibrium is always achieved over the long term with no existence of bubbles (Abelson *et al.*, 2005).

Estimation issues and assumptions

The estimation procedure used involves several econometric measures, reflecting the specific requirements for the OLS method, the Johansen co-integration and the VECM assumptions using time series data. Time series data are routinely used and applied in macroeconomic fields. This is because time is a key variable and most economic, and other time series data are related, often strongly, to recent historic data. Another feature of the time series data integrated into our empirical test is its quarterly data frequency. In particular, to resolve the violation of assumptions, a number of extensive econometric tests were conducted using advanced time series analysis techniques (Croucher, 2017; Wooldridge, 2012).

Multicollinearity is a phenomenon in which two or more predictor variables in a multiple regression model are highly correlated. Multicollinearity issues are avoided by employing a best subset test, using Minitab Statistical Software (Pennsylvania, USA) to identify which combinations of explanatory variables contribute to a high R^2 (Croucher, 2017).

Under the OLS assumption, concerns about autocorrelation with error terms are typically raised. To avoid these, we use the Durbin–Watson statistic (D), which is appropriate for testing the possibility of a first-order autoregressive model. The value of D always lies between 0 and 4. The closer D is to 2, the better the fit of the OLS model (Wooldridge, 2012).

In an OLS model, all random variables in a sequence are expected to have finite variances to ensure a good fit for the data (Wooldridge, 2012). We test homoscedasticity using the Glejser test, which regresses the absolute value of the residuals from the original equation, to test the null hypothesis of homoscedasticity and reject the null hypothesis when the p- value is statistically significant. Further, we test the normality assumption, using the Jarque–Bera statistic. We cannot reject the null hypothesis that errors are normally distributed when it is true. This is in accordance with the theoretical recommendations that lack of bias in OLS be established according to a simple set of assumptions (Croucher, 2017; Wooldridge, 2012).

The p-values are routinely used in null hypothesis significance testing; herein, a significance level of 10 per cent is applied as the threshold value for p (Croucher, 2017; Wooldridge, 2012). The empirical estimation takes the forms of a Johansen co-integration and a VECM, to model the housing bubble test (Hui and Yue, 2006).

To resolve the non-stationarity or unit root problem, the Johansen co-integration estimation requires integration of a number of variables of order 1 at first differences (Wooldridge, 2012). We used the augmented Dickery–Fuller (ADF) test to examine the null hypothesis that a unit root is present in the time series data sample. Furthermore, a key reason for employing a VECM to test for bubbles is the assumption that if economic equilibrium is a condition and economic forces are balanced or in equilibrium, we can conclude there is no housing bubble (Valentine and Garrow, 2013). If the error correction coefficient is negative and significant, the short-term adjustment reverts to long-run equilibrium, thereby suggesting that the house price is always in equilibrium. Therefore, no bubble exists (Wooldridge, 2012).

Moreover, the Granger causality test has been employed to ascertain the variables impacting on changes in house prices (Hui and Yue, 2006). Testing causality in house prices, in addition to correlations via OLS will add greater explanatory weight to the predictors of house prices identified (Wooldridge, 2012).

The variables tested in the unit root test, Johansen co-integration test and VECM, incorporate transformed logarithm values. This is in accordance with theoretical recommendations that the transformed empirical variables might serve as a better indicator for visualization and interpretative purposes (Croucher, 2017; Wooldridge, 2012).

Data sample

The data sample used in this research was taken from ABS, RBA, CoreLogic and the US economic trading website for the period from 1995Q4 to 2015Q3. Therefore, it incorporates the relatively stable economic environment over the past two decades but including the most recent pre-pandemic housing boom started in 2012. Use of these reputable data providers ensures good quality data for our study.

Table I presents descriptive statistics regarding the macroeconomic conditions and housing statistics relating to the maximum, minimum, mean and standard deviation values for the key variables included in the data sample. Moving along the time horizon, the Australian economy enters its twentieth year of remarkable economic growth (Battellino, 2010); indeed, since 1991, the economy has grown in almost every quarter. During the reviewed period, inflation averaged 2.6 per cent, a little above the mid-point of the target range.

Additionally, over the period, the unemployment rate fell substantially, from 9 per cent to 5 per cent, as economic growth supported minimum risk and more people to find work. This benefitted income levels per household, which rose by a cumulative 30 per cent in real terms (Battellino, 2010).

The standard variable mortgage rate is applied in the econometric test. Given the non- availability of an average mortgage rate, this is unavoidable. During the period, although the mortgage standard variable rate reached a maximum value of 10.5 per cent during 1995Q4, there were substantial rate cuts from 2012 to the end of our research period in 2015Q3; reducing rates to as low as 5.45 per cent in 2015Q3, reflecting the government's use of monetary policy to manage inflation rate targets (Battellino, 2010). As the Australian mortgage market relies heavily on variable rate mortgages, variable mortgage loans are subject to high interest rate risk. Financial stability risk is infused as a result of changes to monetary policy (K'fer, 2014). Furthermore, as house prices are directly affected by interest rate shocks, the risk of housing bubbles occurring increases.

Another important variable estimated is AUSHARE. The S&P/ASX 200 share index tracks the performance of 200 large companies based in Australia. Theoretically, positive stock market performance reflects the growth of the Australian economy and increased consumer confidence. Stock market performance is relevant to the real estate market, as stock market performance directly effects changes within it (Okunev *et al.*, 2000). For example, a stock market collapse could lead to economic downturn and financial distress, thereby increasing the risks from a housing bubble.

	Mean	SD	Min	Max
Mortgage interest rate (%)	7.16	1.08	5.45	10.5
Average weekly earning ($)	823.5	191	555.4	1136.9
Home value hedonic index	419.1	162.9	168	729.6
AU S&P/ASX 200 stock market index	4014	1150	2164	6568
Unemployment rate (%)	5.99	1.21	4.1	8.6
GDP (%)	3.24	1.10	1.20	5.40
Population (mil)	20.63	1.74	18.12	23.87
Inflation (%)	2.60	1.31	−0.40	6.10

Table I.
Key macroeconomic and housing statistics (1995Q4 – 2015Q3)

Source: ABS, RBA, Core Logic RP Data and Trading Economics Database

Although it may not capture the performance of the Australian economy fully, CS is a useful statistical measure and economic indicator of the overall health of the economy, as determined by consumer opinion. The data applied in our empirical tests refer to Westpac-Melbourne Institute CS Index taken from the RBA website.

According to the fundamental law of demand, householders' purchases of properties are backed by purchasing power. To include this variable, we use a data series specifying average weekly earnings (AWEs) over the studied 20-year period to perform our empirical estimates. During the study period, the data indicate a continuing growth trend from the end of 1995 until the end of the testing period, 2015Q3. AWEs have increased by 105 per cent since 1995Q4.

As shown in Figure 1, the data used to measure house prices is taken from the CoreLogic Home Value Hedonic Index series (HP) for 1995Q4 to 2015Q3 for Australia nationwide. HP shows prices have increased by 335 per cent over the past two decades. From 1995Q4 until 2012, the home value hedonic index followed a light cyclical trend, and while there was an increase in house prices between 2001 and 2003, there was a mild downturn afterwards. The second growth period started in 2008Q4, immediately after the exogenous financial shock of the global financial crisis and is mainly attributable to the Rudd government's stimulus package. There was then a slow downturn that continued until 2012. The third house price surge then began in 2012, continuing until 2015.

Table II reports the correlations between the selected variables, all of which are expected to correlate closely with house prices. However, strong correlations between house prices and selected economic variables are insufficient to explain house price dynamics, and whether Australia is at risk of a housing bubble.

Results and analysis

Main drivers of Australian house prices

Many of the variables integrated into our econometric test have been subject to large fluctuations over the past two decades and have thereby influenced housing demand and supply substantially (Kohler and Merwe, 2015). This finding echoes the assumption that housing demand is dependent upon typical variables (i.e. real permanent income, demography, house prices and the cost and availability of finance) (Abraham and Hendershott, 1996).

HP

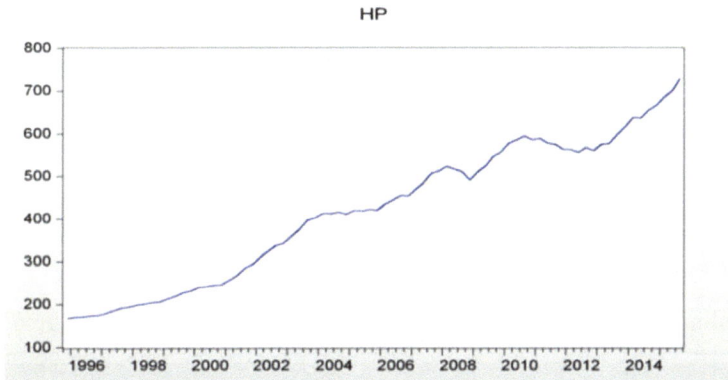

Figure 1.
CoreLogic home
value hedonic index

Source: CoreLogic RP Data

Table III presents the results from the OLS estimation of the main drivers of house prices for the period from 1995Q4 to 2015Q3. All four major drivers are statistically significant, with p-values lower than 5 per cent. The R^2 is 99 per cent, indicating that 99 per cent of the variations in the value of the house prices can be attributed to the four main drivers identified in the model (Croucher, 2017).

Estimations of IR indicate a significant negative influence on house prices, with a coefficient of 4. This result suggests that a 1 per cent decrease in IR could

31

generate an increase of 4 per cent in the housing price index, ceteris paribus. Since October 2012, there were six consecutive cuts to the RBA cash rates within the study period. These shifted mortgage lending rates and had a positive impact on household balance sheets, because of the reduction in mortgage expenditure. The major proportion of mortgage debt expense is positively correlated with short-term interest rates (Koblyakova et al., 2014), and decreased mortgage expenses can improve households' cash "ow liquidities, such that the probability of increased housing demand may be explained by the capital gain effect and large positive premiums over lower mortgage expenses, thereby increasing house prices.

The next variable, the estimate of the Australian S&P/ASX 200 stock market index (AUSHARE) shows a statistical significance and positive coefficient of 0.01, suggesting people are more likely to make property purchase decisions during better market performance. According to rational expectation theory, outcomes depend partially on what people expect to happen. When AUSHARE performs well, households expect economic growth and are confident about capital gains. This triggers a rise in housing demand. Evidence was presented that there is a negative lead-lag relationship between house prices and stock prices in Australia, indicating the existence of capital switching activities between real estate and stocks (Lee *et al.*, 2017).

	Home value hedonic index	CS Index	Mortgage interest rate (%)	AU S&P/ASX 200 stock
Market index Consumer Sentiment index	-0.18 (0.12)			
Mortgage interest Rate	0.31 (0.005) ***	0.02 (0.872)		
AU S&P/ASX 200 stock market index	0.84 (0.000) ***	-0.03 (0.814)	0.11 (0.334)	
Unemployment rate (%)	-0.715 (0.000) ***	-0.001 (0.996)	0.002 (0.984)	-0.777 (0.000)***

Table II.
Correlations among predictor variables (1995Q4 to 2015Q3)

Notes: *Indicates significant at 90%; ** at 95%; *** at 99%

Variables	Coefficient	t-ratio	p-value
CS index	0.22	2.11	0.04**
Mortgage interest rate (%)	-4.0	-4.33	0.00***
Unemployment rate (%)	1.93	1.59	0.12
AU S&P/ASX 200 stock market index	0.01	3.13	0.00***
One lag of home value hedonic index	0.99	88.90	0.00***
Dummy variable D408	-20.07	-2.61	0.01***
C	-12.23	-0.61	0.54
R^2	0.99		
Durbin–Watson	1.93		

Table III.
Main drivers of
Australian house
prices

Notes: *Indicates significance at 90%; ** at 95%; *** at 99%

Consistent with our theoretical hypotheses, interestingly, estimates of the unemployment rate (UNEMPLOY) show an insignificant impact on house prices, with a positive coefficient of 1.93. A lower unemployment rate may alleviate affordability constraints because of the increased purchasing power associated with higher incomes. However, one might ask why an increased unemployment rate would lead to an increase in house prices in our econometric test. One possible explanation is the positive correlation between unemployment rate and interest rates (Table II). High unemployment rate tends to reflect the high interest rate, representing a restrictive investment environment. A rise in the unemployment rate prompts government policy makers to lower interest rates to boost economic growth. Thus, rises in unemployment rate led to lower interest rates and as a consequence increased house prices.

When including CS as an explanatory variable in our econometric model, the parameter estimate shows a significant positive coefficient of 0.22, suggesting higher consumer confidence in the economy and housing market results in a growth in intention to purchase property. Thus, the limited housing stock may face greater demand, triggering higher prices, ceteris paribus (Sivitanidou, 2011). This result reflects the assumption that households apply rational expectations when making property purchasing decisions.

In our econometric estimate, AWE is found to be a positive coefficient, significantly correlated with the house price, suggesting that household owners with higher purchasing power tend to purchase more properties. As AWE is found to have strong correlations with IR, which may lead to a high multicollinearity risk, we exclude AWE from the model but include IR as our main driver of housing prices.

Other housing demand, supply, macroeconomic and demographic explanatory variables, including GDP, population and inflation were found to be insignificant. The results suggest the impact of global financial crisis (D408) is significant to house prices (denoted by HP), and there is a significant positive impact from a lag in house prices (Abraham and Hendershott, 1996). The inclusion of dummy variable D408 is to ensure that the OLS model to test main drivers of Australian house prices meet the Cusum of Square stability requirement in Eviews. It does not reflect Australian house prices in a bubble position. Dummies pertaining to purchases by large Chinese buyers, purchase through self-managed super are also insignificant. This means, Chinese buyers' large purchase activities did not drive Australian house prices during the most recent housing boom (Valentine et al., 2015).

Ordinary least squares assumptions

The checks performed to test the validity of the OLS assumptions involved in the empirical estimation of house price dynamics indicated that the *p*-value of the residuals is 0.97. As this is greater than 0.05, we accept the null hypothesis that the error term is normally distributed. The next piece of data showed estimations of autocorrelation revealed a Durbin–Watson test statistic of 1.93, which is very close to the critical value of 2. Therefore, we assume there is no first order linear autocorrelation in the regression residuals.

The estimation shows the variance inflation factor for the main drivers of house prices is in the range between 1 and 5, suggesting the variance values of the estimated coefficients for explanatory variables are inflated by factors between 1 and 5. Therefore, given the moderate multicollinearity identified, some factors might be deemed slightly redundant. Estimations using the Glejser test show p-values are > 0.05 and are statistically insignificant; therefore, we accept the null hypothesis of homoscedasticity. Original data instead of first difference of explanatory variables were used in OLS test because of their suitability to meet the OLS assumption requirements.

The results of the residual diagnostics show that the assumptions of the classical linear regression model are met. The Gauss–Markov theorem is applicable, and hence the OLS estimators are the best linear unbiased estimators (BLUEs).

Tests for bubbles

An ADF test was conducted to explore the possibility of the stationarity of the variables at first differences. The results obtained reveal that none of the variables are stationary with the exception of the IR. However, significant test statistics were reported for each case when the variables are first differenced. (Table IV). The non-stationarity of data at first difference meets the requirement of further econometric tests on bubbles.

Variables	Level		First Difference	
	t-statistics	*p*	*t*-statistics	*p*
ln(House Value Hedonic Index)	-1.74	0.41	-2.60	0.09*
ln(CS)	-4.25	0.00	-10.49	0.00***
ln(Mortgage Interest Rate)	-3.79	0.00	-5.49	0.00***
ln(Unemployment rate)	-2.18	0.21	-5.13	0.00***
ln(AU S&P/ASX 200 Stock Market Index)	-1.68	0.44	-7.42	0.00***
Notes: *Indicates significance at 90%; ** at 95%; *** at 99%				

Table IV.
Results of the ADF
unit root test

	λ_{max}	Max (Critical Value 95%)	*p*-value	λ_{trace}	Trace (Critical Value 95%)	*p*-value
R = 0	40.38	33.88	0.007**	91.52	69.82	0.000**
R ≤ 1	21.87	27.58	0.228	51.14	47.86	0.024**
R ≤ 2	18.78	21.13	0.104	29.27	29.8	0.057
R ≤ 3	10.48	14.26	0.182	10.49	15.49	0.245
R ≤ 4	0.01	3.84	0.917	0.01	3.84	0.917
Notes: *Indicates significance at 90%; ** at 95%; *** at 99%						

Table V.
Johansen co-
integration results

Table V presents empirical results for the Johansen co-integration test. We identify two co-integration relationships in the trace test, and one co-integration relationship in the maximum eigenvalue test, at the critical *p*-value of 5 per cent between house prices and their main drivers. Our empirical estimate suggests the lag for the first-differenced terms is 4, when using Schwarz Information Criteria. The assumption that all the time series data must be integrated to an order 1 under the Johansen co-integration test is met, and we can therefore proceed to the VECM test for the presence of housing bubbles.

Table V reports the multivariate Johansen co-integration results, together with critical values at 95 per cent. The lag length was determined according to the VAR model, using the Schwartz information criteria. Therefore, a lag length of five was specified.

The results for the VECM test are reported in Table VI below. In all cases, the parameter estimates for the ECT are significant and have the expected negative sign, indicating the speed at which house prices return to equilibrium after a short-term disequilibrium correction. Specifically, the ECT (-1) estimated coefficient is

-0.001, suggesting that 0.1 per cent of a short-term disequilibrium corrects within three months. Accordingly, the empirical results reveal that there are no housing bubbles in Australia because the short-run disequilibrium always corrects over time. Thus, house prices are in equilibrium, and we can conclude Australian housing market is not in a bubble.

The results for the Granger causality test are reported in Table VII. Parameter estimates indicate IR, CS, and AUSHARE, Granger-cause house price changes, reflecting that these macroeconomic variables provide statistically significant information about the future values of HP. Together with the OLS result reported in Table III, the econometric tests analyzed relationships between macroeconomic variables and house prices both at regression and causal strands. These test results indicate the four major drivers identified in our empirical analysis greatly impact house prices.

	Coefficient	p-value	t-ratio
Error correction	D (ln(Home Value Hedonic index))	0.01***	2.62
CoinEq1	0.001		
Notes: *Indicates significance at 90%; ** at 95%; *** at 99%			

Table VI.
VECM result for bubble testing

	Chi^2	p-value	Result
D(ln(Mortgage Interest Rate)) ⇒ D(ln(Home Value Hedonic Index))	19.82	0.00***	Y
D(ln(CS Index)) ⇒ D(ln(Home Value Hedonic Index))	10.40	0.03**	Y
D(ln(AU S&P/ASX 200 Stock Market Index) ⇒ D(ln(Home Value Hedonic Index))	11.94	0.02**	Y
D(ln(Unemployment rate) ⇒ D(ln(Home Value Hedonic Index))	2.56	0.63	
Notes: *indicates significant at 90%; ** at 95%; *** at 99%			

Table VII.
Granger causality test result

Discussion

From a macro-perspective, any reduction in IR significantly influences house demand, and in turn house prices. Thus, changes in monetary policy have a direct impact on both house price movements and housing market performance. In other words, the governments' consecutive cuts in interest rates to manage inflation targets and economic growth estimations, contribute to possible housing bubbles and endanger financial stability.

Notably, the empirical results indicate income and purchase power are key drivers of house prices. Although we have included IR as the key driver in our OLS Model (Table III) because of the strong correlation between income and house prices. However, the data shows that over the past two decades, while income has risen by 105 per cent, house prices have increased by 335 per cent. This is a critical figure, revealing that house price increases exceeded growth in income threefold. This could potentially result in affordability problems for purchasers, which might in turn contribute to declining home ownership, increased competition among house buyers and structural housing problems over the long run.

Conclusions

The primary aim of this paper was to explore house price dynamics and assess the possible presence of housing bubbles in the Australian national housing market. This house price study raises important implications for national economic performance, financial stability and individual wealth management. A combination of rigorous econometric tests was employed using quality data obtained from reputable data providers for the period from 1995Q4 to 2015Q3. Another distinctive feature of the estimation procedures related to the resolution of diagnostic concerns, by applying extensive and advanced time series approaches.

Our empirical findings comply with basic economic trends suggesting households are more likely to purchase properties when interest rates are low, resulting in increases in house prices in such circumstances. Positive CS and good performance on Australian share market, were found to be more likely to result in higher demand for properties, thereby also increasing Australian house prices.

The unemployment rate was also an important purchasing power indicator, although this is likely to be linked to the fact that policy makers reduce interest rate when unemployment rate is high. The findings further suggest the most recent pre pandemic housing boom started in 2012 in Australia does not constitute a bubble, despite the RBA's implementation of consecutive cash rate cuts since October 2012.

The principal contribution of this research lies in its delivery of a comprehensive understanding of Australian house price dynamics and housing bubble literature, based on historical data collated over the past two decades. This study is also the first to analyze the most recent pre pandemic housing boom in Australia. Moreover, the data compiled and models applied are novel raising a wide range of policy implications, e.g. for monetary policy, affordability schemes and indicating a need for other policies to incentivize the construction industry and other industries associated with property. In addition, this study is the first to combine rigorous econometric methods to analyze house price dynamics integrating both correlation and causal perspectives to assess national level data.

These findings are especially relevant to policymakers because they highlight that the economic benefits of house price growth can be channeled into growth in the construction industry, the health of financial institutions and other industries associated with property. This transmission channel is itself governed by the management of significant economic policies, such as monetary policy.

Additionally, the study raises awareness that monetary policy can be something of a blunt instrument when employed to manage the country's financial stability. There is a need to design a balanced and complementary combination of financial policies and monetary policy decision making to improve the country's overall financial health. Key policy implications presented in this research include the need for governmental affordability programmes, especially for young people and first-time homeowners.

Future research might usefully test a broad range of supply factors to establish how they correspond with the country's urban economic policies. Further analysis of the effect of the recent boom in apartment construction might also consider the significance of demographics, such as the aging Australian population. An additional dimension to explore might relate to the possibility of an empirical investigation regarding tests for bubbles using real-time methods. Comparative studies with other countries are also suggested as beneficial. For example, test run of the datasets on other developed countries who also experienced housing bubbles such as the USA, Ireland and Spain aiming to have a falsification and sense check in addition to the understanding of the similarities and differences on outcomes and causes.

References

Abelson, P., Joyeux, R., Milunovich, G. and Chung, D. (2005), "Explaining house prices in Australia: 1970 -2003", *Economic Record*, Vol. 81, pp. s96-s103.

Abraham, J.M. and Hendershott, P.H. (1996), "Bubbles in metropolitan housing markets", *Journal of Housing Research*, Vol. 6 No. 2, pp. 191-207.

ABS (2016a), "Housing finance commitment (owner occupied and investment purposes)", Available at:
www.abs.gov.au/AUSSTATS/abs@.nsf/DetailsPage/5609.0October%202016?OpenDocument (accessed 21 December 2016).

ABS (2016b), "5206.0 – Australian national accounts: national income, expenditure and product", Available at:
www.abs.gov.au/ausstats/abs@.nsf/mf/5206.0 (accessed 21 December 2016).

Adams, Z. and Füss, R. (2010), "Macroeconomic determinants of international housing markets", *Journal of Housing Economics*, Vol. 19 No. 1, pp. 38-50.

Arestis, P., Gonzalez-Martinez, R.A. and Jia, L. (2017), "House price overvaluation in Hong Kong: identifying the market fundamentals and understanding the 'bubble", *International Journal of Housing Markets and Analysis*, Vol. 10 No. 2, pp. 282-304.

Aron, J. and Muellbauer, J. (2010), "Modelling and forecasting UK mortgage arrears and possessions", CEPR Discussion Paper Number DP7986, Centre for Economic Policy Research (CEPR), University of Oxford, UK.

Battellino, R. (2010), "Twenty years of economic growth, address to Moreton Bay regional council", RBA in speeches, available at: www.rba.gov.au/speeches/2010/sp-dg-200810.html (accessed 21 December 2016).

Biggs, M., Mayer, T. and Pick, A. (2010), "Credit and economic recovery: demystifying phoenix miracles", available at: https://ssrn.com/abstract=1595980 (accessed 11 April 2017).

Bleby, M. (2016), "Property now Australia's biggest industry, property council says", *Australian Financial Review*, Vol. 28, p. 39.

Bodman, P. and Crosby, M. (2004), "Can macroeconomic factors explain high house prices in Australia?", *Australian Property Journal*, Vol. 38 No. 3, pp. 175-179.

Bourassa, S. and Hendershott, P. (1995), "Australian capital city real house prices, 1979–93", *The Australian Economic Review*, Vol. 28 No. 3, pp. 16-26.

Case, K.E. and Shiller, R.J. (2004), "Is there a bubble in the housing market?", Cowles Foundation Paper No. 2089, Cowles Foundation for Research in Economics, Yale University.

Chan, H.L., Lee, S.K. and Woo, K.Y. (2001), "Detecting rational bubbles in the residential housing markets of Hong Kong", *Economic Modelling*, Vol. 18 No. 1, pp. 61-73.

Christiano, L.J. and Fitzgerald, T.J. (2003), "The band pass filter", *International Economic Review*, Vol.44 No. 2, pp. 435-465.

CoreLogic (2016), "CoreLogic housing and economic update Nov 2016", available at: www.corelogic. com.au/reports/chart-pack.html (accessed 21 December 2016).

Croucher, J.S. (2017), *Quantitative Analysis for Management*, 4th ed., McGraw-Hill, Sydney.

Del Negro, M. and Otrok, C. (2005), "Monetary policy and the house price boom across US States", FBR of Atlanta Working Paper No 2005-24, available at: https://ssrn.com/abstract=831066 or http:// dx.doi.org/10.2139/ssrn.831066 (accessed 17 April 2017).

Diba, B.T. and Grossman, H.I. (1988), "Explosive rational bubbles in stock prices?", *The American Economic Review*, Vol. 78 No. 3, pp. 520-530.

Fereidouni, H.G., Al-Mulali, U., Lee, J.Y.M. and Mohammed, A.H. (2014), "Dynamic relationship between house prices in Malaysia's major economic regions and Singapore house prices", *Regional Studies*, Vol. 50 No. 4, pp. 657-670.

Fernández-Kranz, D. and Hon, M.T. (2006), "A cross-section analysis of the income elasticity of housing demand in Spain: is there a real estate bubble?", *The Journal of Real Estate Finance and Economics*, Vol. 32 No. 4, pp. 449-470.

Flood, R.P. and Hodrick, R. (1990), "On testing for speculative bubbles", *Journal of Economic Perspectives*, Vol. 4 No. 2, pp. 85-101.

Flood, R.P. and Hodrick, R.J. (1986), "Asset price volatility, bubbles, and process switching", *The Journal of Finance*, Vol. 41 No. 4, pp. 831-842.

Glaeser, E.L. and Nathanson, C.G. (2014), "Housing bubbles", NBRE Working Paper No. 20426, National Bureau of Economic Research, Cambridge, August.

Glindro, E.T. and Delloro, V.K. (2010), "Identifying and measuring asset price bubbles in Philippines", BSP Working Paper, No. 2010-02, Bangko Central ng Pilipinas, Manila.

Harley, R. (2016), "The Australian financial review's rob harley: lessons from a life in property", *AFR*, 19 November 2016, pp. 14-15.

Hatzvi, E. and Otto, G. (2008), "Prices, rents and rational speculative bubbles in the Sydney housing market", *Economic Record*, Vol. 84 No. 267, pp. 405-420.

Himmelberg, C., Mayer, C. and Sinai, T. (2005), "Assessing high house prices: bubbles, fundamentals and misperceptions", *Journal of Economic Perspectives*, Vol. 19 No. 4, pp. 67-92.

Hou, Y.Z. (2010), "Housing price bubbles in Beijing and Shanghai? A multi-indicator analysis", *International Journal of Housing Markets and Analysis*, Vol. 3 No. 1, pp. 17-37.

Hui, E. and Yue, S. (2006), "Housing price bubbles in Hong Kong, Beijing and Shanghai: a comparative study", *The Journal of Real Estate Finance and*

Economics, Vol. 33 No. 4, pp. 299-327.

Kä fer, B. (2014), "The Taylor rule and financial stability—a literature review with application for the Eurozone", *Review of Economics*, Vol. 65 No. 2, pp. 159-192.

Keen, S. (2007), *Deeper in Debt: Australia's Addition to Borrowed Money*, Centre for Policy Development, Sydney, NSW.

Keen, S. (2011), "Economic growth, asset markets and the credit accelerator", *Real-World Economics Review*, No. 57, available at www.paecon.net/PAEReview/issue57/Keen57.pdf (accessed 17 April 2017).

Kehoe, J. (2016), "No more RBA interest cut", *AFR*, 9 October, p. 1.

Kim, K.H. and Suh, S.H. (1993), "Speculation and price bubbles in the Korean and Japanese real estate markets", *The Journal of Real Estate Finance and Economics*, Vol. 6 No. 1, pp. 73-87.

Koblyakova, A., Hutchison, N. and Tiwari, P. (2014), "Regional differences in mortgage demand and mortgage instrument choice in the UK", *Regional Studies*, Vol. 48 No. 9, pp. 1499-1513.

Kohler, M. and Merwe, M.V.D. (2015), "Long-run trends in housing price growth", RBA Bulletin, September.

Leamer, E.E. (1983), "Let's take the con out of econometrics", *American Economic Review*, Vol. 73 No. 4, pp. 31-43.

Lee, M.T., Lee, C.L., Lee, M.L. and Liao, C.Y. (2017), "Price linkages between Australian housing and stock markets: wealth effect, credit effect, or capital switching?", *International Journal of Housing Markets and Analysis*, Vol. 10 No. 2, pp. 305-323, doi: 10.1108/IJHMA-05-2016-0037.

Meen, G. (2011), "The economic consequences of mortgage debt", *Journal of Housing and the Built Environment*, Vol. 26 No. 3, pp. 263-276.

Mikhed, V. and Zemcik, P. (2009), "Testing for bubbles in housing markets: a panel data approach", *The Journal of Real Estate Finance and Economics*, Vol. 38 No. 4, pp. 366-386.

Nanda, A. and Tiwari, P. (2013), "Sectoral and spatial spillover effects of infrastructure investment: a case study of Bengaluru, India", *RICS Research*, Royal Institution of Chartered Surveyors, July.

Okunev, J., Wilson, P. and Zurbruegg, R. (2000), "The causal relationship between real estate and stock markets", *The Journal of Real Estate Finance and Economics*, Vol. 21 No. 251.

Otto, G. (2007), "The growth of house prices in Australian capital cities: what do economic fundamentals explain?", *The Australian Economic Review*, Vol. 40 No. 3, pp. 225-238.

Phillips, P.C.B., Shi, S.-P. and Yu, J. (2013), "Testing for multiple bubbles 1: historical episodes of exuberance and collapse in the S&P 500", Research Collection School of Economics.

RBA (2016), "Table D6 lending commitments—all lenders", available at: www.rba.gov.au/statistics/ tables/?# (accessed 21 December 2016).

Scanlon, K. and Whitehead, C. (2011), "The UK mortgage market: responding to volatility", *Journal of Housing and the Built Environment*, Vol. 26 No. 3, pp. 277-293.

Shi, S.P. (2016), "Speculative bubbles or market fundamentals? An investigation of US regional housing markets", CAMA Working Paper No. 46/2016, Australian National University, July.

Shi, S.P., Valadkhani, A., Smyth, R. and Vahid, F. (2016), "Dating the timeline of house price bubbles in Australian capital cities", *Economic Record*, Vol. 92 No. 299, pp. 590-605, doi: 10.1111/1475-4932.12284.

Shiller, R.J. (2000), *Irrational Exuberance*, Princeton University Press, Princeton.

Siegel, J.J. and Thaler, R.H. (1997), "The equity premium puzzle", *Journal of Economic Perspectives*, Vol. 11 No. 1, pp. 191-200.

Sivitanidou, R.M. (2011), "Market analysis for real estate", *Unpublished Manuscript*, Copyright 2011 by Petros Sivitanides, University of Southern California.

Stevenson, S. (2008), "Modeling housing market fundamentals: empirical evidence of extreme market conditions", *Real Estate Economics*, Vol. 36 No. 1, pp. 1-29.

Teng, H.-J., Chang, C.-O. and Chau, K.W. (2013), "Housing bubbles: a tale of two cities", *Habitat International*, Vol. 39 No. 3, pp. 8-15.

Tsatsaronis, K. and Zhu, H. (2004), "What drives housing price dynamics: cross-country evidence", *BIS Quarterly Review*, pp. 65-78, available at: https://ssrn.com/abstract=1968425, (accessed 17 April 2017).

Tu, Y. (2000), "Segmentation of Australian housing markets: 1989-98", *Journal of Property Research*, Vol. 17 No. 4, pp. 311-327.

Valentine, T. and Garrow, N. (2013), *Economic Context of Management*, 2nd ed., Pearson, Sydney. Valentine, T., Croucher, J.S. and Wang, J. (2015), "Is there a Chinese property splurge?", *Australia and New Zealand Property Journal*, Vol 5 No. 1, pp. 54-57.

Whitehead, C. and Williams, P. (2011), "Causes and consequences? Exploring the shape and direction of the housing system in the UK post the financial crisis", *Housing Studies*, Vol. 26 Nos 7/8, pp. 1157-1169.

Wilson, P., White, M., Dunse, N., Cheong, C. and Zurbruegg, R. (2011), "Modelling price movements in housing micro markets: identifying long-term components in local housing market dynamics", *Urban Studies*, Vol. 48 No. 9, pp. 1853-1874.

Wooldridge, J.M. (2012), *Introductory Econometrics: A Modern Approach*, South-Western, Mason, USA.

www.ingramcontent.com/pod-product-compliance
Lightning Source LLC
Chambersburg PA
CBHW041313210326
41599CB00003B/88